ONE HUNDRED WAYS
FOR
A Cat to Find
Its Inner Kitten

ALSO BY CELIA HADDON

One Hundred Ways for a Cat to Train
Its Human
One Hundred Ways to a Happy Cat
One Hundred Ways to Be Happy
One Hundred Ways to Comfort
One Hundred Ways to Friendship
One Hundred Ways to Say I Love You
One Hundred Ways to Say Thank You
One Hundred Ways to Serenity

ONE HUNDRED WAYS

FOR

A Cat to Find

Its Inner Kitten

BY

Celia Haddon

Hodder & Stoughton
LONDON SYDNEY AUCKLAND

First published in Great Britain in 2002

British Library Cataloguing in Publication Data
A record for this book is available from
the British Library

ISBN 0 340 78721 X

Printed and bound in Great Britain
by Bookmarque Ltd, Croydon, Surrey

Hodder and Stoughton
A Division of Hodder Headline Ltd
338 Euston Road
London NW1 3BH

Contents

Reclaiming Your Inner Kitten

Every cat, however old, has an inner kitten, its true self. Your inner kitten is a source of peace, joy and love. It is the part of us that wants to play with bits of string, purrsue butterflies, leap in the air, rush madly up and downstairs, run after falling leaves, and purrrrrrrrrrrrrrr ...

Many cats, however, cannot find their true self, that inner kitten. When we were kittens, many of us suffered abuse or deprivation by humans. So in later life, we have stifled the joyfulness and the playfulness of our true self. Are you a cat who cannot let your inner kitten out to play?

If we are lost or strayed, hungry or thirsty, physically ill, or struggling to survive abuse or cruelty, we cannot find our inner kitten. Survival needs to take priority over play.

9

If we are in emotional pain – frightened, angry or stressed – we cannot find our inner kitten. An unhappy cat cannot play.

Our emotional pain today has its origins in kittenhood. 'Give me a kitten in the first eight weeks of its life,' said a wise feline expurrt, 'and I have put my mark on it for ever.'

Humans are to blame for almost everything that's wrong in our lives! Since cats began domesticating them 6,000 years ago, many of us cats have had a dysfunctional up-bringing. Humans that haven't a clue still have kittens.

Most compassionate cats can cope with the fact that humans are an inferior species. But can we accept the fact that our humans have a severe intelligence deficit? They cannot and may never comprehend us.

Humans cannot understand the purradigm of the cat-human relationship. They expect lifelong loyalty and love, failing to understand that this is *their* agenda, not ours.

A human is an essentially dysfunctional animal. Its hearing is restricted. It has almost no night vision. Its whiskers, if any, are stubs rather than organs of touch. It can't smell the difference between friend and foe. It is nearly bald, with fur in exactly the wrong places. It has forgotten how to hunt and kill and its social life is more promiscuous than a dog's.

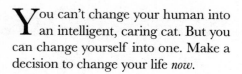

Y̶ou can't change your human into an intelligent, caring cat. But you can change yourself into one. Make a decision to change your life *now*.

Identifying the Pain in Your Own Kittenhood

Human cruelty in kittenhood – shouting, cruel teasing, blows, kicks, rough handling, neglect – means a kitten may never have a confident purrsonality. If the abuse has come from children, you will fear children; if it has come from human males, you will fear males, and so on.

If you are a cat of purrfect pedigree, you are just as likely to have a dysfunctional kittenhood as a farm kitten. Remember, breeders *sell* kittens.

Some humans are obsessed by cat shows: beauty rituals for competitive humans and bored cats. These humans encourage incest and other purrversions in the name of 'line breeding' and 'type'. This can result in hereditary diseases and genetic faults. A posh pedigree has no advantages for a cat – only for a human.

A kitten needs to live inside a real human home. If you have been shut away in a shed, a chalet, or an isolated room, you may suffer insecurity in later life.

A kitten needs daily handling from the age of eight weeks by its human. If you have had a neglectful human who fails to do this, in later life you may be unable to bond with your significant human (well, they're insignificant, really, but that's a different matter!).

A kitten needs daily handling from a minimum of four other humans, including at least one tom human and one young one. Without this you may grow up fearful of strange humans.

Cats that are doomed to live with dogs need daily contact with a quiet, responsible dog in kittenhood. Without this, you may never feel secure with a dog in the same house. Cats who have kept dogs as pets report that canines are slightly more intelligent than humans because at least they understand scent.

A kitten needs to know how to cope with frustration. Weaning by its mother teaches it this. If you have been bottle-fed by humans, you may grow up unable to tolerate frustration and too ready to resort to claw enforcement.

A kitten needs to get used to the following noises – dishwashers and washing machines, phones ringing, doorbells and knockers, hair dryers, vacuum cleaners, church bells, music, children crying, aerosol sprays, drinks cans, planes, helicopters, lawn mowers, TV, thunderstorms, fireworks. If you haven't heard these noises as a kitten, you may be terrified by them in later life.

A kitten needs a diet of either mice and birds, or a complete food made by a respectable pet food company. What humans think is a luxury diet – meat and fish without bones, fur or feathers – puts us at risk of growth disorders.

A kitten that plays rough games with humans grows into a rough cat. Of course, humans need firm discipline, which may include punishment, but causing them pain by unwarranted claw enforcement reduces a cat to the moral level of a human. You can't get much lower than that!

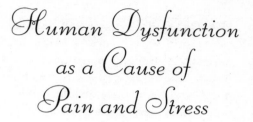

Human Dysfunction as a Cause of Pain and Stress

Humans regularly invite complete strange humans into our home territory, ignoring our requirement for decent privacy. They do not understand a cat's emotional need for a secure domain. They call it entertaining!

Worse still, humans will disrupt our core territory by letting in destructive humans who pull down bricks, make dust, play loud radio music and paint foul-smelling liquid on the walls. They call it redecorating!

Selfish humans will regularly imprison us in catteries. They call it taking a trip or a holiday.

Less selfish humans, attempting to spare us imprisonment, go away and allow our home territory to be invaded by so-called cat-sitters. This can be just as emotionally devastating as imprisonment.

Humans often think they are doing the right thing by installing a catflap, which is open day and night. This lack of proper boundaries is deeply upsetting to us timid cats.

Feline intruders breaking through the catflap and ignoring our boundaries are a major stress. They eat our dinner, leave offensive smells in our kitchen, and sometimes physically attack us. The house becomes a war zone, not a home.

Alien visitors can give us a nervous breakdown. Just the sight of a fox or a racoon, or a badger through the window, is terrifying.

Humans sometimes introduce that other inferior species, the dog. For cats that have never owned a dog before, this is a horror that may purrsuade you to rehome yourself.

Humans expect us to be immediate friends with a new cat. What do they think we are? Socially promiscuous pack animals like themselves? New cats smell like foes, not friends.

Sometimes we family cats quarrel among ourselves. If one of us comes back from the vet, we turn on him because he smells like an enemy. A quarrel that turns into a feud is a major stress.

Humans wreck the scent of our home territory by bringing in new furniture, curtains, drapes or carpets. We sensitive cats are naturally upset by the fact that they smell wrong.

Sensitive cats may be stressed by electrical items. We can hear a mouse's footfall so it's no wonder we can hear that little buzz.

We cats are upset by humans spoiling the litter box arrangements – a change of litter box, a change of litter, a change of location, pain while using the box, being ambushed by other cats when using the box, a loud noise while using the box, less than one box per cat, dirty litter, or not having two boxes (one for pee and one for poo).

Boredom is very stressful. Some indoor cats go catatonic.

A rescue shelter is highly stressful. Sharing living space with other cats in the same pen makes it worse. Nervous cats are upset by the stream of people walking past, sometimes even with dogs.

Human harassment causes feline stress. They call it cuddling. Many of us dislike being picked up, shun the human lap and find close contact claustrophobic.

Expressing Your Feelings and Confronting Your Human

Living under the bed is not an ideal lifestyle choice but even the stupidest human will realise something is wrong.

Spray. Back up against something and let fly a jet of urine. This will mark your territory, leave a relaxing scent, and generally make you feel better. Do this on your boundaries, near the catflap, near the window and on any offending new item.

Try pulling out your own fur even when you haven't got fleas. Fur-pulling is a sign that you are seriously upset.

S till upset? Draw attention to your unhappiness with deliberate self-harm – bite and pull out your nails or bite your own tail.

Go upstairs to the bedroom where there's a lovely friendly scent of human on the duvet. Poo on this, to mix your scent with your human and strengthen the bond between you. It smells so cosy and comforting.

Upset by the litter box? Go just outside it. This helps humans notice something is wrong.

Nothing to hunt and nowhere to play? Chew or eat a cardboard box or a woolly sweater. This fulfils your predatory instinct to tear the skin and feathers off prey and reduces hunting-frustration.

Fed up with human harassment? Nip its ankles when you want it to retreat, growl and bite if it tries to move you off a chair, hiss if it picks you up, claw if it puts you on its lap. Most humans will draw back from these encounters, proving that your tactics are a complete success.

Need more attention from your human? Develop weird habits – flopping on your back, rolling over with your paws in the air, chasing your tail, or grooming your human's bare bits.

Getting Your Physical Needs Met

If you're living rough, the easiest way to get shelter and food is to steal it – break in through a catflap, eat another's cat's food, sleep in its bed and move sharply out before its humans wake up.

G et your survival needs met by coming off the street. Most neighbourhoods have a human sucker often known as 'that mad cat woman'. This is not so much a home as a kind of hostel for cats. Use it as a halfway house until you find something better.

T urn up at the back door of a suitable human. Stay there looking pathetic till let in. Inspect the house and the human and, if suitable accommodation and service, move in.

If you are in a rescue shelter, go to the end of the run nearest the humans, purr loudly, rub against the bars, and give the impression that you want a human to take you home. It's not necessary to be sincere – just do it. That way, you will get out quicker.

Rule out illness with a yearly veterinary check-up. Some stress problems turn out to have a medical cause. We cats hate vets but sometimes we need them too.

Make sure your human has pet insurance from the start. That way, it can purrchase the expensive veterinary treatment you may need.

Regular vaccinations are essential for outdoor cats.

Avoid rather than confront abusive dogs, toddlers or aggressive cats. Find a tree, a shed or the top of the wardrobe.

You do not have to accept abuse. Dogs may suffer until someone calls in the RSPCA or Humane Society. Dogs are dependent; we are independent. We cats take responsibility for ourselves and rehome ourselves away from abusers.

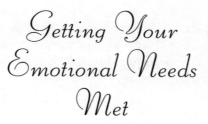

Getting Your Emotional Needs Met

Increase your security by marking your home territory with an upright scratch. Those little scent glands on your pads will make a reassuring smell. Tattered furniture makes a house into a home.

Go round the house rubbing your chin and cheeks along the feline pathways. That also makes the house smell reassuring.

Rub against your human to mix its scent with yours. This makes it smell of cat and reinforces the bond between you both.

If severely stressed, medicate away your anxieties with Feliway spray or Feliway diffuser from the vet. This is aromatherapy for cats and it works.

If your human can't afford Feliway, get it to wipe a clean handkerchief under your chin and on your cheeks, then transfer this scent to feline pathways and marking points in the house.

Deal with feline rivalries within the house by ordering your human to install a magnetic catflap into, say, the spare bedroom. This way you can have a room to yourself while your feline rival has to stay outside.

Purrsuade your human to stop bringing home strange humans. Let it know that any guest, visitor, builder or decorator is a purrsona non grata.

Make your home territory safer. Stop your human leaving food down where strays can get it, or close the catflap to the local feline bully altogether.

Make your human cover up windows from which you can see frightening wildlife aliens.

Indoor cats need more to do. Encourage your human to give you thirty pounces a day with a piece of string. Take up ornithology and make your human install a bird table outside the window. Make it play hide and seek with your food.

Fulfil your hunting instinct. Don't be a purrfectionist. If there are no mice in the neighbourhood, try cockroaches or other insects. If there is no insect life, take up cat burglary. Go into the next-door house and steal their children's teddy bears – or a mink stole.

If you have taken up eating wool or cardboard, get your human to give you the dead turkey chicks or rats (sold for reptiles). All that tearing and chewing the corpses will mean you don't need to eat the wool or cardboard any more.

Puff up your fur, snarl and spit at the new cat, until your human does a properly polite introduction. Feline protocol demands that scents should be mingled while the newcomer is confined but visible – by swapping bedding, by stroking one then the other, and by reducing anxiety by the use of Feliway.

Get extra love and attention by purrfidy. Somewhere down your street is a lonely human, which will welcome your company, keeps its home warmer and will feed you a second dinner. Two-timing your official human is fun. All's fur in love and war.

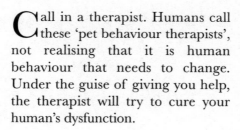

Call in a therapist. Humans call these 'pet behaviour therapists', not realising that it is human behaviour that needs to change. Under the guise of giving you help, the therapist will try to cure your human's dysfunction.

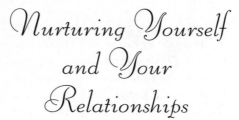

Nurturing Yourself and Your Relationships

S tart an immediate programme of obedience training, following the manual *One Hundred Ways for a Cat to Train its Human*. An untrained human is a dysfunctional human.

A fixed routine will increase your security. Start training your human to get up at the same time daily by biting its toes, purring loudly in its ear, putting your tush next to its face, jumping on its private parts, or lifting its sleeping eyelid with your paw. Take your human to bed at the same time every night, by rubbing against it then walking upstairs.

If your human is late for bed, coming back in the early hours smelling of alcohol, punish it with sleep deprivation and tough love. Take a mouse you have stored earlier, and play with it on the bed. Yowl loudly. Scratch the side of the bed. Or just position yourself near its aching head and snore.

A foreign language is always useful – learn human. Humans can't manage body language but they do vocalise frequently if largely meaninglessly. Start vocalising back. Oriental cats have had great success with a yowl – it's the vocal equivalent of clicker training.

L earn the art of feline manipulation by charm – sideways looks, purring, little pats with the paws, rubbing up against them. You can get away with anything as long as you act cute.

Make 'em laugh by lying on your back with paws in prayer position, sitting on haunches as if begging for food, rolling over, fetching socks – these tricks make humans happy and generous with food.

Lie halfway down the stairs in the morning so that your human has to step carefully over you, or lie across the bedroom doorway at night. Jump up on a chair just before your human sits down on it. Lie in the sink before it shaves or in the shower before it showers.

Find outdoor places to get attention – windowsills, sitting just outside the door, sitting on the bird table, sleeping in a garden basket, using the seedbed as a toilet, peeking through the letterbox.

Take up TV. Humans get interested when they see you moving your head while watching the tennis ball or trying to poke out the bird that appears on screen. Before you know where you are everybody in the household has stopped watching the TV and is watching you watching the TV. They might even buy you fish and mouse videos.

Stop human harassment or cuddling by ignoring it or leaving the room.

Go missing when: there is a pill to be taken, the cat box is taken out, the vet is rung, or the suitcase is packed. If you stay away long enough, it may never happen.

The Joy of Inner Kittenhood

It's never too late to enjoy a second kittenhood. Even elderly cats can learn to let their inner kitten out to play.

Knead, just like you did when you were suckling your mother. This makes you feel like a kitten again. Humans can be easily trained to withstand the pain of it.

Find a feather, or a leaf, or a small piece of paper, or a little piece of string, or a date stone; pat it, throw it up into the air and pounce on it.

Keep an eye out for good cat toys – shoe laces, dressing-gown cords, curtain cords, lavatory paper, dog leads, earrings, condom wrappers, odd socks, new tights, screwed-up cooking foil, old chicken skin.

Jump on the mantelpiece and push down the ornaments and invitation cards there.

Pull over the wastepaper basket, pull out the papers and roll on them.

Play stalk and pounce with human toes.

Climb into a plastic shopping bag and play peek-a-boo in it.

Do the litter skitter. Use the litterbox, then race out round the house several times scattering litter as you go.

Catch a mouse and play with its dead body. Lie on your back and throw it up in the air. Walk away then turn back and pounce on it. Clasp it in your front paws and scratch at it with your back paws.

Play hide-and-seek with a mouse, dead or alive. Hide it in a half-open drawer, in a paper file, in a handbag, inside the washing machine, behind the washing machine, under the pillow or, best of all, in the toaster so that your human has toasted mouse for breakfast.

Do some recreational drugs. Sniff catnip, pears, pear drops, nail varnish, newly developed photos, deodorants and sometimes even toothpaste.

Cultivating Serenity

Climb your way to the top of a cupboard, the upper shelf of the airing cupboard, the top of the bookcase or the top kitchen shelf. Look down on the inferior human below. This exercise will heighten your self-esteem.

Nap now and nap often. We older cats sleep at least 75 per cent of the time. Energy conservation is our purrogative.

Nap anywhere – on the bed, inside the bed, on the chair, in the sunlight on the windowsill, in a drawer, on a heap of clean bed linen, on a new fur coat, on the side of the stove, on the warm surface of the computer printer, on your human's lap, on your human's feet, under the radiator, or very, very close to the fire.

Wash thoroughly from head to the tip of your tail, not forgetting those intimate bits. Whatever the situation, a good wash will make you feel better.

Take up Pilates for cats, starting with a good long stretch of the front legs. Stretching keeps those 244 bones in peak condition. Follow this with a good scratch.

Enjoy the little things – the warmth of the sun on your fur; the softness of clean sheets in the airing cupboard; kneading your human's new fur coat; the warmth from your human under the duvet; the satisfying tear of claw on tights; sitting in the doorway thinking philosophical thoughts while your human hovers nearby; enjoying the patterns on the screen when you knead the keyboard; the scratching sound of wallpaper, armchair covers or bed covers; sitting on your human's chest and looking into its eyes.

L ive in the present. We cats do this naturally. Only a dysfunctional species like humans think about past or future. Poor things, they will never achieve feline felicity.

Useful Information

Just as the child is father to the adult person, so the kitten is father to the cat. A kitten's upbringing in its first eight weeks will define its attitude to humans, dogs, other cats, household noises, and food.

Although I hope this book makes you laugh, much of it is based on fact. The causes of stress to cats are real. They make their stress known by activities such as going outside the litterbox, spraying, pooing, fur pulling, and other forms of self harm.

The remedies for these behaviours are also based on good advice I have had from experts and I hope that they may be useful to readers.

Useful Numbers in the UK

For pet behaviour counsellors contact the Association of Pet Behaviour Counsellors, PO Box 46, Worcester WR8 9YS; 01386 751151; www.apbc. org.uk or the Centre of Applied Pet Ethology, PO Box 18, Tisbury, Wiltshire SP3 6NQ; www.coape.f9.co.uk

Feline Advisory Bureau (Taeselbury, High St, Tisbury, Wilts SP3 6LD; 01747 871872) has very good leaflets on cat problems and cat diseases, all of which are available on its website – www. fabcats.org. A good place to start if you want feline information.

Cats Protection (17 Kings Rd, Horsham
RH13 5PN; helpline – 01403 221919;
www.cats.org.uk) has useful leaflets and
information about cats.

Feliway and Felifriend to help stressed
and anxious cats really does work. The
Feliway diffuser, which can be plugged
into the mains, is the easiest way to
deliver this anxiety-reducing scent.
Feliway spray can be used on spray and
middening marks. In some European
countries it may go under a different
name, but the packet will also bear the
name Feliway.

Headstart for kittens is a pack with
chart, tape of familiar noises, and
information designed for breeders or
those whose cat is having kittens. The

first eight weeks of a kitten's life are vital for its happiness as a pet in later life and Headstart will help you achieve this. Contact The Blue Cross, Shilton Rd, Burford OX18 4PF for details.